The Alibi

Rob Kersley

ArtNut

Copyright © Rob Kersley 2024

The right of Rob Kersley to be identified as the author of this work has been asserted in accordance with sections 77 and 78 of the Copyright Design and Patent Act 1988.

Email: rlkersley@aol.co.uk
Website: www.robkersley.uk

Published by ArtNut imprint of MA Publisher (Penzance)
Email: mapublisher@yahoo.com
Website: www.mapublisher.org.uk
Released on August 2024

Print on Demand books are printed in each region of the continent listed and distributed there through the print on demand chain.
Australia | Canada | Europe | UK | USA

ISBN-13: 9781915958129

All rights reserved. No part of this publication may be reproduced, stored in a retrieval system, or transmitted, in any form or by any means, electronic, mechanical, photocopying, recording, public performances or otherwise, without prior written permission of the copyright holder, except for brief quotations embodied in critical articles or reviews.

Disclaimer:
All expressions and opinions of the work belong to the artists/Author and MAP & ArtNut does not share or endorse any other than to provide the open platform to publish their work. For further information on MAP policies please email: mapublisher@yahoo.com for further information and submission guidelines.

Cover designed by Mayar Akash
Cover image: by Rob Kersley (Penzance, Cornwall)
Copy edit: Liz Kersley
Typeset in Times Roman, Title font: Arial Black

 Paper printed on is FSC Certified, lead free, acid free, buffered paper made from wood-based pulp. Our paper meets the ISO 9706 standard for permanent paper. As such, paper will last several hundred years when stored.

Rob Kersley's poetry offers a fresh and moving take on everyday life. His poems are full of raw emotion and sharp insights into personal and social issues. His writings are both beautiful and relatable, making his reflections deeply touching. This book is a must-read for anyone who enjoys heartfelt, gutsy poetry that speaks to the heart of the world around us.

CHRIS JONES
Senior Leader at Gateway Church, New Zealand.

Rob Kersley's work is openly emotional with acutely felt moments of joy along with its counterpart, pain which are both expressed in a number of the pieces, the more complex of which are profound and multilayered. The intimate imagery and symbolism of his poetry is both accomplished and often deeply moving.

MICHAEL GINSBORG
Artist and Lecturer, London.

Dedication

To the children to whom the baton will be passed,
with no small degree of apology but with eternal hope.

Acknowledgements

My heartfelt thanks to photographer and friend, Michelle Blaken, who once again undertook the sizeable task of photographing my sketches for this book with professionalism, sensitivity and passion.

To Mayar Akash, my publisher and friend. When I didn't share his confidence in me, he remained inspirationally steadfast.

And to my wife and best friend, Liz. Thank you for everything.

Contents

Dedication	5
Acknowledgements	6
Introduction	9
This Changes Everything	10
Census 2521	12
Hold A Mother's Hand	14
Any Man	16
This Time V France	17
England Day!!!	18
Maistre Blue	20
Rethink, Rebuild	22
The End Of The World	26
Evicted Arachnid	28
You're The One	30
The Services	32
I Think...	34
The Eve Of Post-Denial	36
Long Sentence, Together	37
Down To The Shore	38
Cash For Lies	40
Absent, I Found It	41
Of Valentine's Born	44
Transparency At Last	46
I Awoke On Thursday	48
Light Will Come	50
Mariupol Mother	52
The Basics	54
Land Of Plenty	55
Dolmen Dunce	57
Missed Calls	60
The Pack Travels Light	61
The Wreckers	62
Just Eat	66
Poor Froggy	68
How I Feel	72
Cracking It Alone	73
Every Nereid And Venus	76
Washed In Time	80
Lest We Sleep In Late	82
National Express	84
The Dawn Of Recalibration	86
Delilah	88
9 To 5	90

About The Author	92
Also By Rob Kersley	93

Introduction

Welcome to my third book of poems compiled from work that originally appeared under the title, Honddu Valley Herald.

I sat down to begin the process of organizing the poems into this single volume in April 2024, although I originally wrote and posted the individual pieces between March 2021 and February 2023. This was the post-pandemic period for the most part, and a returning to "normality"; a re-emerging from the dark days of our isolation.

In many respects, I believe that we learned a good deal in those Covid years. I believe that we emerged more enlightened, more aware and more sensitive. But the established, overarching pressures somehow remained stubbornly in place. The same, seemingly immoveable power still prevailed with the same commodities and currencies, and we continued to function within the same primary structures. Our development would therefore have to content itself with merely shining an unflattering new light on these basic principles, and we would have to find new ways to navigate and make sense of some harshly exposed realities, some unpleasant details and some dubious compromises.

The challenges that we knew were coming our way before the pandemic were still present of course. In fact, we could now see them looming larger than ever. The enormous work that was required to address global poverty, inequality, human rights and of course the big one, climate, were to become even thornier and encircled by ever more extreme flurries of proposals, counter-proposals and on occasion, denial. Each opinion would gather giddying momentum within the insulated vacuum of its very own echo chamber. What exactly was happening here? Returning to our new normal, we couldn't pretend that we didn't have a glorious opportunity, a once in a generation moment to re-define our priorities and re-align ourselves.

As I re-read the pieces that I first produced during those disjointed, transitional years, it struck me that one day when our derelict and out-dated monolithic structures are finally pulled down, those years will be forensically scrutinized. They will be interrogated not only for the harsh realities that were undeniable by then, but also for the desperation of a generation who had enjoyed a life in relative peacetime with all the fruits of their forefathers' labours. How we, as a collective, resisted any significant change. How every conceivable distraction, every misleading conflation was seized upon for justification and used as an excuse. If there was one thing that we held in abundance, it was cover stories.

 Welcome to The Alibi.

This Changes Everything

Easter:
And we sent cards with images of the
Hope, new life and rebirth,
That changes everything.

Saturday:
And this beautiful young woman
And her proudly attentive husband sit the prescribed two metres opposite me in the cool, Cornish sunshine
And chatter while I lose myself in grateful wonder,
At my little girl and son-in-law.

Then:
A little nervously, she clears her throat before rather formally
Thanking me
For the Easter card.
Then, failing to suppress a determined grin, reaches into her handbag
And hands me a black and white image.
It could have been a cave painting,
Mystical, otherworldly.
Disproportioned, smeared, vague and watery.
The image of new life at just twelve weeks
In the silent midst of its slow, rapid, complex development.
A human pupa in her very body residing,
A chrysalis of loving cells dividing,
A beautiful essential thing
With all its essential things in micro, cellular form,
It's wonderful!

...And then:
Unable to hug, I shriek, and stare through happy, salty tears
From ultrasound image
To beaming parents and back again at this
Wonderful miracle. This
Hope, new life and rebirth;
This changes everything.

Census 2521

Glazed over for a few dazed minutes, she was brought back to the moment by
The thin, clean electric tone,
As the hallway door opened and another entered her white room,
Then marched past her without acknowledgement
And into the adjoining brightly lit space.
The frosted, opaque door slid silently behind him and sighing, she focused
For the umpteenth time on the prompting cursor
In the pale blue screen on which it traced.

One page and one question remained,
The same one with which she had struggled in 2511.
There was a time she would have openly questioned them,
But those days she had explained away as a momentary phase, a lapse.
Citing some unresolved family difficulty that she kept concealed perhaps,
To create maximum impact
For when deployed in the event of such emergencies.
She had been allowed to leave, but she knew
That anything she now said or wrote or did would be
Held up and scrutinized for any ambiguity
Or suggestion,
That she was anything other than
Fully compliant.

The cursor blinked with increasing impatience in the corner of the box.
Only one word was required and only one was permitted.
Ten years ago she had berated herself privately.
Having an inner debate, come argument, come rant;
Trying to justify before finally, in a collapse of the brittle fortress of her self-delusion;
Flailing as she implored with her subconscious,
Whaling silently and citing the countless external factors,
The sheer size and domination of the machine she found herself within,
And the extraordinary lengths to which it would go,
Made it impossible surely, for her to write the word as honestly
And as starkly as it had screamed at her every waking moment since.

And here she was again,
Ten years older,
Ten years wiser,
Ten years braver; eyes watered as she looked to the frosted door
And the shape of her civil partner wordlessly moving around on the other side.
He operated with such certainty, so seemingly in sync.

cont.

He appeared so much to be forged of this age,
Swimming with the current,
Talking the talk,
Quoting the approved, carefully casual rhetoric,
Running with the pack,
Crudely concealing a skittishness
Agreeing, supporting, defending,
Denying.

When the form had arrived and the document auto- unzipped
The timer had begun counting down.
And now, nearly two days later
Only thirty or so minutes remained before the deadline,
And if left blank, that in itself would surely give them all the ammunition they needed.
They would read into that, as they presumably had
For so many of those who had tried
But failed to wade against this surging invisible tide.

Her fragile, frightened fingers trembled on the key pad.
Time was running out and was being replaced with a knowing
Deep inside her,
Or felt at least, a growing
Sense of inevitability
That courage would again fail her.
Reluctantly, predictably.
Head hung in resignation,
She typed;
HAPPY.

Hold a Mother's Hand

If I could hold her hand today
It would be enough,
To feel as I've seen,
Behind glass, on a screen.

If I held her hand tomorrow
Everything else could wait.
And the world might stop for just a minute,
Becalmed by the warmth of love within it.

If I could have held her hand yesterday
And felt that bond,
Never separate thus far,
Separateness can't be what we are.
As from the tropics to the winter lands
And coastlines to the hinterlands,
Some surviving better than others,
This world of children with all its mothers..
Reach out,
Be bold,
There are hands to hold.

The Alibi

Any Man

Any man
Who lived, as he was dealt,
To follow a path
And before it, knelt.

Any man who worked
With what he found was his,
Through eyes that knew of nothing less.
Who learned quick, the characters in play,
To recognize on stage, the cast,
As scene by complex scene rolled past.

Any man who sought to find safe harbour,
For him
And for his lifelong partner.
Overcompensating for his human failings,
When all things weighed
Upon the scales,
Those stacked on his side of the railings;
Privilege for which his price was duty,
Authority for responsibility,
Satisfaction from generosity.

And any man so proud of all his children,
That his resistance to this age, forsaken.
Only to learn, he could have freely gifted,
As much as would be finally taken.
Who made complete, that world of his
Albeit, in an era he found so strange,
Stepped willingly onto every stage.
Within a life he could not plan
A footprint lost in seas of sand.
No more, no less
Than any man.

This Time v France

There will be no chic Champs-Elysees this time:
No upturned collars grinning through nimbus ribbons of Gitanes,
Melting into grey / white Parisian skies
And espresso laughter over bleating Deux Chevaux
Echoing between ornately turned balconies.

This time it's, *"purement commercial".*

No gallant, crazed cockerels
Let loose,
To hug the twenty-twos.
Nor swaying shoals of Bretons;
Bouteille in one huge mitt,
The other around a beguiling, smiling daffodil-head.

This time, with as much at stake
As ever, to take stock.
This meeting of Celtic cousins will be the jolting, trapezius shock,
As loose and opposing tight-heads lock,
Taking the brunt of a sixteen-man Gaelic grunt.
Bellowing in opposing strange tongue, the rallying call
From the giant blue wall,
And heaving shirts of red up front.

This time, they are meeting a team,
Who are building something very special.
This time, they are meeting a team,
With their entire nation urging them on.
This time, they are meeting a team,
Even greater than the sum of its carefully fashioned Welsh parts.
And led into the Paris night by Alun Wyn,
Who better,
To carry the common dream of thirteen million
Impassioned Welsh hearts.

England Day!!!

I think we should have a bank holiday
And the PM does as well.
To celebrate him ingratiate The Sun,
While the rest can go to Hell:

I don't mind that Ireland's hung out to dry,
Nor that Scotland's had enough.
Doesn't matter to me, that the nurses can't cope,
Their pay cut don't seem rough!

And I've forgotten the thousands dead and gone,
Whilst dear Boris ducked and dived.
Don't care that he broke his lockdown rules,
Since the majority have survived.

What we want is another bank holiday!!
...Seems I only have to ask.
And now Covid's barred from the pubs and bars,
There's no need to wear a mask.

To idolize the best team in Europe,
I'll even don a Three Lions blazer.
Support a *Planet Football OBE,*
Call it,
"The Order Of the Laser".

So let's take the day off, if they win,
Spend the whole day in our beds.
Pretend nothing is amiss at home,
While the rest of the world
Shake their heads.

Maistre Blue

It's not those shades of blue reflecting the racing skies above the Cape,
Flecked with white stallions, billowing beyond the Brisons,
In diminishing ribboned blends of teal and Prussian;
That, if I were tall enough to see beyond the limitation of this horizon,
To stretch, unbroken from where I stand,
Across the midnight blue Atlantic..
To the steel blue Island of Manhattan.

Neither is it, the steady stairs of blue/purple bells near Trink,
That carpet the steep rise between the trees that lean
To stare back at Penbeagle,
And beyond St Ives to the sweep of Godrevy.
Below skies of choughs and crows
Like tumbling scratches in murderous ink.

But the clanging blue that strains the head,
Seeps from every sorry word that's left unsaid.
The blue of what's ignored, unread.
The truth of minds and hearts that bled.
Too tame?
Too tired?
Too bored?
Too scared?
Now flood our space and time instead.

Blue stains that won't wash easily
From the chalk of land
Nor weight of sea,
Malignant ideology.
And knowing, that this democracy
Elects liars for themselves to serve.
As blue as Joseph de Maistre's words,
That people get the leaders
That their countries do deserve.

Seland Newydd, Pwllgloyw, Honddu Valley. Rob 2013

Rethink, Rebuild

Ironically, it was my neighbours who'd,
When we first moved here
Told me colourful tales,
Of the storms and the gales
We could expect to see first-hand.
Living, as we now do
On the very first
And last step of dry land.

Young Rio and his wife India, were forthcoming with anecdotal advice,
And seemed at once in tune
As they traced the ancient narrative of this corner
Bearing its post-industrial face.
They stepped in time with the pace of this place,
And their house;
A solid square of granite,
Centuries old, looked for all the world
As though successive eras of windblown erosion
Had slowly led
To the gradual exposure
Of a building,
Honed in the deep rock bed.
The surrounding landscape welcoming it,
Wrapping it up in its arms as an organic cornerstone.
Exuding a quiet identity,
The reassuring solidity,
From the neat, colourful garden that spoke of peaceful contentment,
And Cornish hedges trimmed,
That sheltered turquoise moss-covered trees from the wind,
And borders
For all vibrant things, brimmed.

But the aspect of their home that they seemed
To be most proud:
Was the iconic shallow sloping roof,
Its most recent makeover involving hand cut stone and slate.
Sheared and shipped from Delabole,
The rows of differing shapes and shades,
Designed with the help
Of the craftsman they had discovered.
"Does all the high end work

cont.

In the most select neighbourhoods.
He's re-roofed the homes bearing wealthy complexions
Town houses in Pall Mall
With royal connections."

The lead work had ornate little finishes,
Trimmed into curves and decorative flourishes.
Fleurs de lys dotted here and there,
Signature details of precision and care.
And this wonderful roof was finished
With handmade, clay ridge caps.
"Decorative & functional" ...some with animals faces,
Dates and names would tell,
Of its proud craftsman,
And the homeowners themselves.
Thus presenting proof, that this one year old roof
And my neighbours,
Would be indelibly laced
Into the fabric of this place.

For once, the two weather apps agreed,
For usually, one would contradict the other to some degree.
But a storm was gathering,
The tempest that the weather experts had predicted for some time
Its whip to crack,
On Truthwall's exposed back.

No one escaped completely.
We were all traumatized, relatively.
But a never to be seen again,
Missing in action wheelie bin,
And a broken limbed apple tree left prostrate on the path
In the terrible aftermath,
Was nothing
Compared to the losses suffered
By Rio and India.

Their amputated roof drew new
Unwanted attention,
As did the surreal image of an entire roof section,
Now lying like a broken body near the bus stop.
The uninvited storm had performed its worse deeds,
Heavy stone slates blown like dandelion seeds
Timbers and all.

Cont.

Leaving the pair
To stare
From their soaked bedroom carpet
At the unstable, flimsy fabric
Of their world
That otherwise,
They would never have seen.

I know,
It's hard.
But honest to God,
This savage storm has shone
An unwelcome spotlight,
On frameworks and the reliability of structures.
Leaving us reeling with uncertainty
And facing the undeniable reality,
That if we don't all rethink,
Redesign and deal with
The fundamental flaws and imbalances laid bare,
The next one will be worse, it's true.

Superficial dressings
Evidently, won't do.

The End of the World

Why does the sun go on shining?
Why does the sea rush to shore?
Don't they know, it's the end of the world?
Cause they don't care much, any more.

Try to dismiss all the data,
Try to deny the extremes.
Don't they know, it's the end of the world?
It faded as they counted beans.

Try to dispel all the warnings,
Then undermine the experts.
Don't they know, it's the end of the world?
But the party was the best ...and worst.

Why do we trust politicians?
Why, when such lies are exposed?
Don't they know, it's the end of the world?
Their lust for power, unopposed.

For all of the pledges in Paris,
Forgotten, as yesterday's news.
Don't they know, it's the end of the world?
Each shameful state stares at, their shoes.

The Office For Zero Emissions'
Tokens of pseudo concern.
Don't they know, it's the end of the world?
Reduction targets crash, and burn.

Will we miss the last chance, of reversal?
Will the money machines, have their way?
Don't they know, it's the end of the world?
They sure won't be the ones, who'll pay.

Our children in four generations,
Could inherit a wasteland for sure.
Will they know, the last hope for their world,
Had slipped out while we held, the door?

Bethel Baptist Chapel, Pwllgloyw, Honddu Valley

Evicted Arachnid

If I twist my legs sideways
I can thread like lace through the narrow space
Between the end bath panel and the skirting's base.
Keep an eye on my exit
Just in case.
It's good to get out,
But I'm nervous.
Self-conscious,
At my dust brown mass that's gained apace.
This fissure never felt
Like it was such tight a place.

I was hoping,
They wouldn't be around,
That as I emerged, I might be allowed
To at last stretch these legs without being found.
But no...
The taller, silver-haired one was actually sat on the loo.
I made the man jump, I'd swear on it too,
He actually leaped off the seat as I scurried into view,
And stopped one step short
Of the smooth, hairless sort,
Strange rows of odd toes
Wrapped in skin bound so taut.
His eyes nearly popped out
Yes, his shock was implicit
But the noise that emitted
(And I know this sounds grim)
Suggested
That I helped to loosen things
For him!

He froze.
I froze.
My eyes fixed on him and his on me.
Then he disappeared, for which I was humbler
But when he came back
He came back with a tumbler.
I knew it, he was going to do that thing,
Trapping me under the glass,
Well not this time buddy, cont.

Not me, not..
"Clump!" ...I was trapped
And yes, there's the card being slid underneath,
I hate this!
Tips the glass the other way up and comes right up to it,
Staring at me.
What a strange, ugly creature he is.

He makes an echoing noise with his mouth
Before the other one appears.
Two of them peering, gawping,
Makes me so mad.
And in spite of my action,
Scrabbling at the glass
I fail to get traction.
My two front legs stretched up,
Frozen, petrifaction.
They stare and point with their horrible, thick, fingers.
Then down the stairs we go and out into the cool dark.
He tilts the glass on the path and I sprint away fast
Past the tall shafts of grass,
Crafts like sail boat masts,
To find safety.
The safety
Of shadows at last.

Where on God's earth am I?
He's squatting,
Squinting like a lost dime
Perhaps he remembers me from the last time,
Perhaps he's impressed by how much I've grown,
How much thicker more hairy, more hefty and wider.
But perhaps he should look behind the bath panel
If he wants to see a really impressively, menacing, spider!

You're the One

You're the first face I see each morning,
And the last voice I hear at night.
My smile you match,
My breath to catch,
And the palm my hand holds tight.

The best friend I waited long for,
Many hills and bridges crossed.
That true light found
On St Buryan's ground,
I still search for, when I'm lost.

The Services

Tiredness can kill, I thought
When I saw you at the services,
Treading water in the Costa line.
Cheeks puffed,
Your shoulders fell.
As a sigh slipped silently.
Quiet as the rooted tree
That old trustee
You longed to be.
For a moment
Your best face turned to me,
But as oak would be
You didn't see.

I glimpsed you at the services,
Tracing the turns,
Drawn by the miles,
Sketched debris piles.
Washed over by stationary glazed automotive vials
In ever more upwardly mobile styles.
Centred from reservation exiles,
On congested tarmac aisles.
Lifestyle statement, sound bite smiles
Heads for all answers,
Hold inadequate files.

I watched you at the lip glossed services,
Gazing through shoals of your species,
Enshrined via prisms like turning leaves,
Consigned down a slipway of churning breeze,
As one, enticed by marble lures,
Funnelled, corralled, it arrives,
At Burger King
And Accessorize.
But designer holes consign her awkward knees.
Perhaps,
She's rebelling (or trying).
It can't be easy,
When everyone on her phone
Seems to be lovin' da party,
Just like she.

cont.

The Alibi

I overheard you at the services,
Reflecting on the chapter left behind,
The scenery flashing by.
Sure, you couldn't just open the door,
Didn't feel you could break,
Until we all broke.
Then silently anxious that the objective might fall short
Of the spot lit anticipation of magnified thought.
Endless day to sleepless night,
We were both holed up,
Mid-story.
Journeys you couldn't write.

Yes, I saw you at the services,
But not sure you were between locations this time.
Just hope this constant striving
Isn't actually your destination
...Or mine.

I Think...

I think...
I know...
  I shun,
  I doubt.
  Maintain the space and insulate,
  Keep everyone's heat out.

I think...
I know...
  But slip,
  Face down.
  Demand empathy I'd never show,
  When *they* were on the ground.

I think...
I know...
  I point,
  I blame.
  From the centre of my world,
  I find the view's always the same.

I think...
I know...
  My script
  Ingrained.
  And since I'm numb and deaf and blind,
  I'll never have to change.

Lower Chapel, Honddu Valley — Rob 2014

The Eve of Post-Denial

In those final, hedonistic days
Of disposability,

The Myth Of The Individual
Teetered, precariously.

Although in its shadow
We'd been kept shameless,

After it collapsed,
Our kids would blame us

For choices made,
When there was no planet B.

Long Sentence, Together

Joined at the hip, we fumble
  and stumble through this jungle like the wounded,
    disgruntled and humbled but grumble,
      half blind, thoughts jumbled
        and mumble rumours to the deaf,
disillusioned, displaced and bereft;
  negotiate the best bits and landfill what's left,
    but lie foetal as spoons in quilted rooms,
      tuned to the moons before the sun looms
        and all too soon
when shackled we plead,
  independently defiant to heed,
    yet inter-reliant to feed,
      individual in spirit
        but together indeed.

Down To the Shore

Follow me down to the shore my friend
To where there's no debate,
Of *who* and *why*
And *must* and *not*
With the dread that it's all too late.

Take me down to the shore again
From the tensions in this land,
To see once more
The tamed wild sea
Caress the quiet sand.

Lead me there, this Christmas Eve,
We'll dream beneath blankets of heather,
Where the harmony
That I still recall,
Might return to us all forever.

Cash For Lies

Would you send me a shiny, new one pound coin
Every time that the sorry man lies,
And I'll set it aside
In great piles of wealth,
Just to see what the sum of it buys.

I might save up for gold painted wallpaper,
Embossed curtains and pelmets with ties.
Or bid on his old
Brexit battle-worn bus,
To find out if its promise still flies.

He's so moved by the nurses and front line workers,
It brought tears to his crocodile eye.
That's why he removed
Every barrier of safety,
Would he "*rather see bodies piled high*"?

"*There's no time to waste! ...Yes, it's one minute to midnight!*"
Into folk with short memories he piles.
Just two years ago
He was a Telegraph hack,
Writing trite, laddish climate denials.

How does he expect us to all stay so decent,
When this man, without shame never tries?
Perhaps he'd rather we all
Just kept counting those coins,
And make hay from his fading disguise.

Absent, I Found It

Back there;
That place was
As a woman robbed of girlhood.
Faded, peeling makeup
Applied with a developer's trowel,
Over what developed
From a fixed grin,
To a grimace,
To a scowl.

We were robbed again back there
Earlier along this journey.
Second time for us both,
We hadn't learned.
But this thief hadn't claimed to be a soul mate
Before cashing it in,
Pulling the rug and wrecking every priceless thing on it.
This was another violation,
We were similarly trusting.
Not nearly suspicious enough,
Not cynical enough,
Not sceptically tuned
To know we had to guard those precious things.
Relative loss
Is an open wound.

In just fifty years or whenever
(However time runs),
I won't be here.
But how grateful am I, that I then found this place;
Her solidity,
Unselfconsciously unapologetic
Sincerity.

When I'm absent
It's only the individuals I miss.
Collectively, reluctantly strapped-in
To the deafening fairground ride.
Buckled-in,
As slaves to a hidden establishment,
Trapped by a sort of misplaced nostalgia.   cont.

Heroically intransigent,
Vehemently denied
But meekly resisted.
A longing for something that really existed.

Well, I found it my friend.
It is real.
It does exist, just as we'd all imagined.
And I'm here for a while,
Foraging for words to describe
Her brilliant skies,
The million smells,
The abundant orchards of good
That exists here.
The acres of time and patience
And goodwill that grows here.
And so grateful am I,
That I found her,
To wonder at it all together.

Of Valentine's Born

In awe, and more
Of Valentine's born
Of heart, knows love won't thrive
Inside.
Then act,
Not shirk
The endless work.
Her self to give,
Denies the hurt.

I stared,
She slept.
No tensions kept,
In quiet repose. Of nil regret;
The crystal clearest conscience deep.
Resplendent, in as out
No doubt,
From all that well-earned
Beauty sleep.

Intuitive mind,
Discreetly brave,
Seems every day,
No task too grave.
Who knows that love can't thrive inside;
In awe
Once more,
Of Valentine's born.

The Alibi

Transparency At Last

We partied
All through that year
'Til
The mourners had gone,
And when
The whistle was blown,
Said,
"Let's all just move on".
We thought
No one could touch us,
Left
No watch on the bridge.
Then,
Avoiding their questions,
Had
To hide in a fridge.
'Cos I'd
Sacked the dissenters,
Made a
Ring round my throne.
To
Appeal to the gutter,
Had
To toss them a bone.
Yes, we
Danced round the headstones,
No
Corruption was spared,
And when
Nobody said much,
We
Guessed nobody cared.
Next, we'll
Throw our net zero
Right
There, under the bus.
Have to
Dream up some reasons,
Hope
They're selfish as us.
Ms Eunice

cont.

Screamed a warning;
Of
The future, she'd chime.
Need
To time our announcement,
Maybe
Wait a short time.
Put the
Squeeze on more families,
Via
Fossil fuel heavies.
Then we'll
Come to their rescue,
And
Bin the green levies.
The oil
Men hold the slush fund,
They're
Our backers as well.
We'll pretend
To stay distant,
But
We'll see them in Hell.

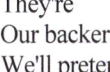

I Awoke on Thursday

I awoke on Thursday, in '39,
Heard the bullets rip through Warsaw.
Friedrich told me that he didn't want this,
Destroying lives by the truckload.
Heike said, "This is sheer madness",
And Jurgen cried, "This is not who I am".

I awoke on Thursday, in '74,
Saw the blood-soaked streets of Saigon.
Chinh told me that he didn't want this,
Destroying lives by the truckload.
Tuyen said, "This is sheer madness",
And Kim-ly cried, "This is not who I am".

I awoke on Thursday, in 2003,
Saw our own bombs killing Baghdad.
Phillip told me that he didn't want this,
Destroying lives by the truckload.
Shirley said, "This is sheer madness",
And Gareth cried, "This is not who I am".

I didn't want to wake up this morning,
Didn't want to see poor Donetsk.
I thought we said that we didn't want this,
Swallowing lies by the truckload.
Thought we'd agreed that it's sheer madness,
I've no idea who we really are.

Light Will Come

Throw open the curtains in Moscow.
Please, tear down St Petersburg's blinds!
Let the sun light the truth for their people,
And liberate their shackled minds.

Give Russia the courage of Kyiv,
As defiant, impassioned she stands.
And perhaps we might yet see this monster,
Made to pay for the blood on his hands.

He's aware that the truth will condemn him.
Only darkness enables his sin.
But the seams of his reign are in tension,
Perhaps that's where the light might get in.

Mariupol Mother

Somewhere her teachers have taken up rifles.
  Sometimes just twelve is no longer her boy.
    Somehow her new life is born to dark shelters,
      Mother would weep, but the river's run dry.

Somewhere cold terror is gripping her nations.
  Sometimes great courage is drawn from her home.
    Somehow her peace is the last thing we'll die for,
      Mother kneels down midst the shelling, alone.

Somewhere her flowers are gifted on door steps.
  Sometimes her breakfast's delivered to bed.
    Somehow not one of us chose our own birthplace,
      Mother thinks only devotion, instead.

Somewhere The Devil's appeared in broad daylight.
  Sometimes every disposition might pray;
    Somehow protect your poor children from horror,
      Mother of God, please drive Putin away.

The Alibi

The Basics

Take one little infant Putin,
To a sandy, Sennen day.
Add a tablespoon
Of a clear blue noon,
And add a half a dozen waves.

Then walk with the infant Putin,
To the soft sand water's edge.
Kneel beside him too,
As, excited through,
His tiny heart pounds in his head.

Now balance the infant Putin,
Upon your surf-waxed board so tall.
While he grips the rails,
Steer him through the tails
Of small white horses, as they fall.

Choose a wave for the infant Putin,
And push his board to catch the bowl.
See the thrill thereof,
As he learns to love,
Something that he can't control.

Gallop! Lift your tender fledgling,
Seize each moment, make them tell.
So he breathes your light,
Feels this love ignite,
And maybe save the world from Hell.

Land of Plenty

We've got plenty of men,
Dressed in plenty of suits, some
In trainers for shoes now and Doc Martin
Boots. And there's plenty of cars here,
No shortage of phones. There are plenty of websites,
The sky's full of drones.

We've got plenty of drapes,
Above plenty of floors. There
Are plenty of windows and plenty of
Doors. And there's plenty of screens,
Where we idolize thrones, then like kings, blame the hardship
On those without homes.

There seems plenty of fracking,
And oil wells we're planning. But we're
Causing more storms now and even more
Famine. We hear plenty of excuses and weak
Alibis, and shed loads of pretending
In barrels of lies.

Though there's plenty of children,
We're not always that fussed. Dare we drink to their future,
Or just toast our own past? We've got
Plenty of views
To select what we see, or delete consequence
As reflections of Me.

We had plenty of luck,
Things we couldn't have planned; A secure loving home,
Not sold on to Rwanda. When *Homes*
For Ukraine is but a hashtag that teases, barbed wire
Only bridged with
Unattainable visas.

There were plenty of years,
But we skipped the revisions, so there's barely the time left to mend
The divisions. There are plenty of folk,
Who can't draw the right lots but their fate is ours too, when we
Join up the dots.

cont.

Last week, plenty of dirt,
Just re-shaded our car. These fine grains beyond borders,
Blew right in from afar. There seemed plenty of choice,
But the hour is so late as the dust bowls and deserts,
Now colour our fate.

I still remember the line
When we all became gentry;
Let every home be a castle, in this land of plenty.

Dolmen Dunce

So I visited the stones
Beyond Madron's lichen, heather and granite boulders.
Stepped across the rippling carpet,
Zipped up coat, double fleeced and with hunched shoulders
Against this feral wind that rushes through.
That's bent its trees,
The characters, the settlement,
And shaped its narrative;
Its history too.

I arrived at the stones
At a time convenient to me.
I assumed, you see
That just as Neolithic shadows cast
By their twelve thousand lunar years amassed,
Their watch extends to those who pass,
Enlightening any
Who dare,
To ask.

I met with the stones
At Lanyon Quoit,
Estimating that they'd seen perhaps
Four hundred and eighty new generations.
I actually counted them with the stones;
Four hundred and eighty who were cleverer than previous
Mothers ...fathers.
Four hundred and eighty
That have come,
And four hundred and eighty new versions
Now gone.

I sat with the stones
Like my last day at school,
Or the first.
But having accumulated more baggage than I'd realised,
Each answer, demanding more,
Disguised;
You get my drift, I couldn't stop.
Think I might have talked there
And listened,   cont.

Quite a lot.

I visited the stones
But came home none the wiser,
Except perhaps some deepening comprehensions,
That whether or not I accept
My intellectual limitations;
I am part of something
More vast, more complex,
More glorious and more grand,
That my chink of brief perspective
Can possibly command.

And you know,
What will make
My end of term report
Even worse...
Is that the more I'm schooled
In the ways of the world,
The less I seem to understand.

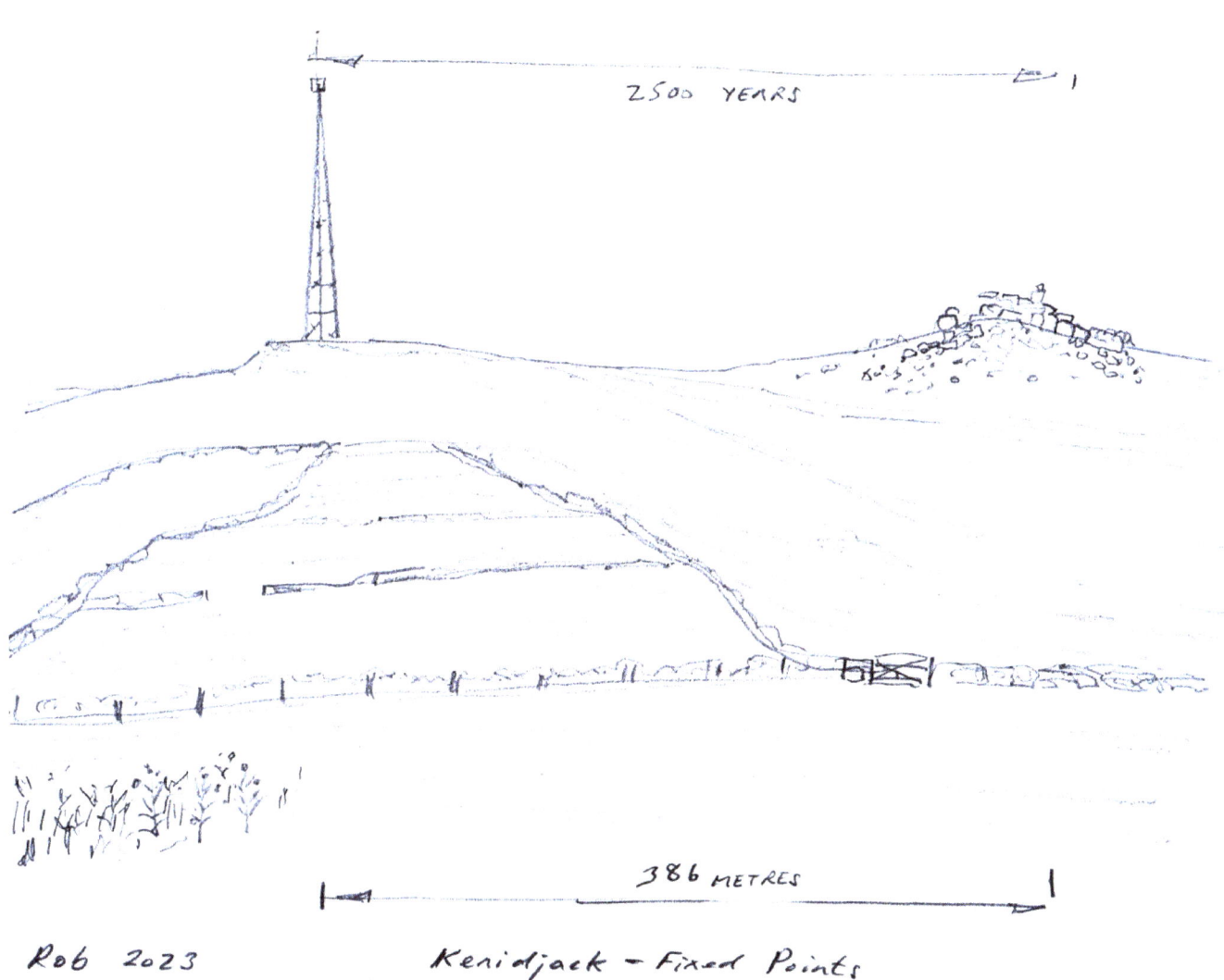

Rob 2023   Kenidjack - Fixed Points

Missed Calls

The still, small voice
  That comes and goes.
    When signal's weak,
      Reception tends
        To not make clear, stuff I'd rather hear.
          The problem's at the other end.

The still, small voice
  That comes and goes.
    "Yeah, you tried again!
      ...Lost track of calls.
        I'm all good though. Just busy, you know...
          Was expecting someone else, that's all".

The still, small voice
  That comes and goes.
    "You're breaking up...
      Look, never mind...
        Not in the best place. Just in case,
          Can you call me back? ...Yeah, anytime".

Whose is that voice
  That comes and goes?
    Don't give a thought
      To those missed calls.
        Cool as it gets... *"I've no regrets"*.
          But that still small voice
            Knows me too well.

The Pack Travels Light

Without these two eyes
There'd be nothing to see,
But the vacuum of light
Of post-integrity.

And without censorship
There seems more I could say,
But that ceiling is glass
And this floor falls away.

Without taking part,
I'd kill democracy.
And if I bury my head
It's a fait accompli...

So if I turned off my hearing
Would there be no din?
Can I bypass my conscience
To eradicate sin?

There's no food bank on my street,
So where is this poverty?
And where there is no black voice
Racism ceases to be.

There's no dust bowl in 'Spoons,
So just where is this drought?
And no famine in Whitehall.
What's the fuss all about?

Since I can't buy a test-kit,
There can be no Covid.
But there's a pack I could run with,
As long as I don't demur it.

'Coz the pack lives in fear
Of its own,
Of the night.
So, discarding impediments,
The pack travels light.

The Wreckers

The Wreckers:
Are nothing new.
They existed in bygone Kernow
Where they built imitation lighthouses
Which were designed
To guide and entrap
The ever-vulnerable seafarers.
The Wreckers sought to isolate and expose,
To lay bare and disarm the naive and unsuspecting.
They were ruthless and unscrupulous,
Taking lives,
Any lives,
Plundering lives,
Ruining lives.

Their prey:
Through squinting, red-raw, salt-stained eyes,
Involuntarily shivering,
Shuddering breathing,
They would navigate the inky waters in that often invisible,
Shifting, narrowing corridor between the freezing,
Seething, mountainous oceans of the open sea
And the jagged black rocks of the coastline,
Equally deadly
And potentially seizing.

Lighthouses:
They existed but the differences
Between the genuine and the imitation
For witnesses,
Were subtle,
Virtually imperceptible.
Invisibly diametrical when viewed
From the chaotic melee,
They appeared to be genuine and reassuring beacons
Through the lashing rain,
The screaming gale,
And stained anguish of subsistence
...Particularly to those who didn't even know
Of the imposters' cloaked existence.

cont.

The Brexit period:
This was not the endgame ...neither was it the opening frame.
It was crafted after a sustained period
Of cheery and
Relatively calm waters.
Peacefulness,
Not of myriad proportions,
But with memories foreshortened
The comfort bar was set higher
Than any previous working generations
Had been able to aspire.
Then came came the sudden,
Inexplicable,
Disorientating hardship of austerity.
The relative storm,
The unexpected gale.
That acrid cloud of clarity's pollution
Was immediately followed
By the all-too-easily digestible solution,
The guiding lights of The Wreckers.
The Brexit period wasn't the beginning or the end,
It was the set-up.
It successfully isolated and exposed its subject,
Laying bare and disarming it
For what would follow.

Their victims:
They will deny the existence of The Wreckers.
They will not have the facts,
Nor their motives to act,
Or the choices they made challenged,
...Nobody needs that.
That
Will be for their future generations,
Who will shake their heads at
The naivety and brutality,
As through tear-blurred eyes,
They read of the wholesale waste,
And the sheer evil that was cradled.
Of how Brexit unfolded
And then what Brexit had enabled.

cont.

Wrecking:
It's an evil game alright
...But this game's
Not a new one
And now The Wreckers are in clear sight.

Just Eat

Don't peel,
Don't dice,
Don't chop.
Just Eat.

Don't cook,
Don't look,
Don't stop.
Just Eat.

Don't scrub,
Don't clean / prepare.
Just Eat.

Don't give,
Don't share, don't care.
Just Eat.

Don't run,
Don't walk, pick up or talk.
Can't sleep, won't weep,
Don't bleat,
Repeat.
   Just work ...and work ...and work ...and work,
   And shop and click and taste,
   Then waste.
Don't stay fresh-faced,
Just cut and paste;
It's sink or swim deceit,
Just Eat.

Don't mess / protest,
No plan, no less.
Can't ask,
No mask,
The past, recast.
   The dye, steadfast,
   Too fast to last.
   No link, don't think,
   Don't pause,
   Just Eat.

cont.

The Alibi

The snare is strung,
For some, no rung.
No home, just street,
No bed, no sheet.
    Just point and shoot,
    Don't help,
    Just Eat.
No hug, no rug,
Just bare concrete.
    Can't feel,
    Won't heal,
    Just crusts and peel.
No shoes, bare feet,
Don't stop,
Just Eat.

Don't grow / evolve.
Don't solve,
Just Eat.

Poor Froggy

If a careless frog leapt into a pan of boiling water,
Water so scolding that every nerve was lit,
Like a furnace
To the finely tuned, cold blooded creature,
That its tiny pulse would quickly quicken, as natural balances cease.
The delicate, ultra-sensitive, perfect skin would dissolve,
Leaving only flesh cooked to a plasticky rubber
And bones reduced to skeletal fibres,
Brittle and delicate as amphibious peace.

If it found itself in a place so hot,
A lot so fraught to distort its thought,
And evaporate memory
Of all it was taught.
Sacrifice subconscious,
Accelerate time,
Annihilate sleep.
And pile its days in a never ending heap, of faster and faster, and faster and faster
So much faster.
Until everyone, every role and every word
It used to understand was suddenly
Unrecognisably,
And irrevocably blurred.

If it found it was suddenly to be a slave,
Being led to a cell,
To leave its dreams neatly folded at the door, with its liberty.
Embrace captivity,
In the name of what? More productivity?
More choice?
More *freedom*?
Less conformity?
The innocent frog
Would gasp, it would shudder
And leap right out the boiling water.
Tell this new order
Where to stick its opportunity.

But see how,
If our poor frog finds itself instead, cont.

The Alibi

In a skillet of tepid water:
Never more comfortable in its very own, private, new pool.
Proud, perhaps protective, or even possessive of his new cool.
Ignoring an instinctive unease with the distant fire,
Suspended as he is, in a frame
Over a steady, progressively, intensifying flame.

Then watch now, as heat is carefully and gradually increased.
A temperature change just slow enough as to be unperceivable,
Especially as our little friend is distracted;
Bedazzled by his new palace and its many accessories,
But it's getting pretty warm now or is it me? Warmer still then, and still poor froggy
Doesn't give a thought to the heat of its grey matter, once comfortable.
There just isn't time all of a sudden,
Chooses to not see how all this started.
Turns a deaf ear to the roar,
Blind to the trend,
Ignores uncool forecasts,
In denial of the end.

Soon enough, confusion abounds,
Steam and bubbles surround,
As views become polarised
And skews sight and sound.
Until nothing is moderate
And not what it seems,
In this, his new normal, cauldron of extremes.
He reaches for the rim, red hot bars of his prison.
In his hall of strange mirrors,
Three-sixty degree prism.
Social media harvesting
Nine pound a gallon capitalism.
When image
And pleasure
And conscience collides,
Reality TV, his plaything
Induced suicides.
How'd it change?
What's the link?
He's too frazzled to think!
A world away now,
From the certainty and shade
Remembers the glade where he laid
Mighty oaks.   cont.

Rob Kersley

He chokes
Red hot steam,
Slay the wokes.
Blames any unknown
Entity that somehow provokes,
The laughing flame it fans,
The coals it stokes.
To the end, he'll deny.
Truth and logic, he'll defy.
His last utterance is a lie that
...He finally croaks.
   Poor froggy!

How I Feel

I don't know how to feel
about losing something i didn't see

I don't know how to feel
she embraced her place like you and me

I don't know how to feel
when she was clearly given more

I don't know how to feel
because she gave without keeping score

I don't know how to feel
I thought we are all born just the same

now I know just how i feel
my heart just sobbed to me in pain

Cracking It Alone

Like asking a spaniel to do a self-portrait,
On a skateboard
With a crayon.
Or convincing her,
Those driving tips
I gave,
Was just me playin'.

Or spinning out of control
In a social role,
Staying, *Natural*
As I could.
But getting strained and bent
As Kevin Costner's accent,
When an Aussie plays
Robin Hood.

Priceless apologies I should have made,
But tripped,
Misformed the words.
When those halves you said,
You shared,
Instead,
Felt suspiciously
Like thirds.

The constant benefit of the doubts,
The other cheek
She'd turned now cries.
As cherished hope concedes
That amassed good deeds,
Would remain,
Unpaid goodbyes.

Then park that Hummer up tight
And trap that Leaf,
No-one's getting out
Without us.
Some karma accounts
(And that),
Might be in the black,

cont.

But their burden's
Just enormous.

So...
As lone campers
Wrestling frame tents
During a force twelve
In Kidwelly.
How can you
Crack an egg
With
Just one hand,
Like
Jamie Oliver does
On the telly?

Every Nereid and Venus

We stood as sibling bronzes before Nereid
Behind Cardiff's Friary Gardens,
Transfixed.
Awestruck, floored
But,
Understated.
Coarse cut,
...Captivated.

Said how we'd never felt such beauty.
"She looks so strong!
Such life,
So light.
Such joy,
Just right."
But oh boy,
How must the chisels
And hammer blows have hurt her.
Each rasping file,
Worked-over to create this polished perfection.
Honed wonderment,
Her creator's own reflection.

"It was great to see you,
To spend some time,"
Priceless.
Priceless moments:

"And there,
Up close I could see the fine details,
Imprinted as features etched into the surface of your face.
Squinted troughs across your forehead,
And weathered cheeks
Like the ripples of low tide,
Lit, like
Low-light peaks,
Where the agony of love was pulled away
In the undertow and hence,
Worked over by tidal events.
Non-scripted in the scroll,
Testament to the toll,

cont.

Investment of the whole
Evolving pupa of your soul."
These, I cannot see in your email, or your text.
I don't feel them in my stationary rear-view mirror,
Engines-off queuing.
There, every faceless silhouette is culpable.
Every other citizen, responsible
For every post to stay afloat,
The nearest boat,
Imploring vote,
Emoji-cloaked
Anonymity of the masses
With its solemn word,
Trampled in the dusty grasses
Behind the jittery stampeding of the herd.

"No, I need you here,
Close enough to touch your breath
And hold a gaze that's
Real enough
To see me too,
Reflected in those eyes
Of hazel, brown and glacial blue.
Who knew my life would mirror yours,
My miracle, yours.
Pure chance, our lesson, your version, same classroom,
Different doors.
Every scar exposed.
Every line
And every track."
Then...
I'm in awe,
-Captivated.
You're stronger than you feel.
And those knocks,
Those endless hammer blows
And chiseled pain, that cut with care;
They created something awesome,
Like a pharaoh beneath your shield I swear.

Transfixed,
Up close and personal.
Before all these people,
All these works of art,   cont.

Every Nereid in this defiant city.
Every Venus de Milo in this tortured land:
"I Need you!
Up close
You're beautiful.
I need you up close.
...There!
...You're beautiful.
I can't help it,
I love you."

Washed In Time

Staring down at the remote
That just turned off the news,
Mid-sentence.
This, our twice daily service
Minus hard, wooden pews;
Repentance.
"It's stopped raining".
Chest rising, then pauses as it gathers,
"...Think I need a walk", she sighs
In dove white peaceful feathers.
Find ourselves gliding past the slanted field
And blasted granite spoils
That yield to stilled,
Victorian Get Rich Quick statues of
Hard, wild sabred foils
From scarred child laboured toils.
Now protected, sanitized, heritage monoliths
To what my species will do.
"Don't be sad", whispers the sea,
"Try not to be sad.
I will wash you in time, I promise, you'll see.
I'll wash you too, in time".

Turquoise, streaked in blue-green tin-washed,
Painted cliffs,
Plummet into an indigo-ultramarine surge
That breathes quietly now,
Post-storm.
Chest rising, then pauses as it gathers
Before dragging itself off the rocks
In dove white peaceful feathers.
Her hand finds mine,
Cold fingers intertwine.
"Don't be sad", whispers the sea,
"Try not to be sad.
I will wash you in time, I promise, you'll see.
I'll wash you two in time".

Cool moonlight through the open window
Catches her cheek
As she rolls toward me.

cont.

Like some dream had told her,
Grips a handful and pulls the duvet
Tight around her perfect shoulder.
As events on repeat,
Reflecting in the shallow pools of patchy, thin sleep.
Chest rising, then pauses as it gathers,
Before letting go the body
As dove white peaceful feathers.
The Atlantic still rolls from behind the old mine.
Warm fingers intertwine.
"Don't be sad", whispers the sea,
"Try not to be sad.
I will wash you in time, I promise, you'll see.
I'll wash you all in time".

Lest We Sleep In Late

Lost friends for words, no song,
No birds.
Dead boys like toys, red eyes,
White noise.
The feedback fades, cold steel
Invades.
We slept in late and sealed
This fate.

A mortar's scream, this view,
Obscene.
Barbed wire re-counts, its bodies
Bounce.
Screams in the smoke, on tears
We'll choke.
We slept in late and sealed
This fate.

Just numbers soon, nostalgic
Tune.
Dry mouth, then worse, antacid
Bursts.
Why them not me?
Could judgement be;
We slept in late and sealed
This fate.

Whose poppy's this who dares
To kiss
A German brave, some
Russian's grave.
Just who decides what hand
Divides.
We slept in late and sealed
This fate.

So leave the pod to plead
With God.
Then shock and awe Donetsk,
And poor

cont.

The Alibi

Baghdad, Helmand on our
Command.
We slept in late and sealed
This fate.

Lest we forget, or better
Yet,
Slay beasts of sin that lurk
Within.
And vow no more to close
The door,
To sleep in late and seal
Our fate.

National Express

There are armed guards on the bus
As we blaze through the days
With relentless intent.
Through burned out communities,
Smouldering factories, charred wreckage of schools,
And the last of the libraries
Where their legacy was piled high
And set ablaze.
Dissent was dealt with by a rifle butt,
So we sat,
Heads down,
Knotted gut.
I had used my sleeve,
To clear the heavy condensation
From the glass to see
What the chanting was all about.
Picket lines of every worn cog in the machine that once
Proudly provided
Essential care and support,
All but conquered, divided.
Sure, we had choices
But those three Main Drivers just kept rotating;
Laziness, Selfishness and Greed,
On a mission to undo,
To re-write,
To unravel,
And bring everything to its knees.
Environmental protestors drowned out
And left choking in our wake.
Squinting through the belching fumes
At our all-new trendy plate;
   CL1M4TE LE4DER.
Incompetence personified by the three by two jammed
Beneath the steering wheel to keep us all at full throttle
No matter what
...And for God's sake, for what?

cont.

My current account is suffering,
Goes out faster than it comes in.
And those savings? ...Long since vanished!
Not a penny left in the tin.
No, don't let me be a hoarder,
Withholding kindness in and out.
Let me graduate to Spendthrift,
A degree in losing count.

Because these days don't feel exactly
Like goodwill's raining from above.
Yet in our hearts, we all have plenty,
And there's
No credit score in love.

I mean some days don't feel exactly
Like grace is raining from above.
Perhaps when hearts are totally emptied
We'll find our way back home
In love.

The Dawn of Recalibration

If I close my eyes, or if I
Squeeze them open,
In the maze of the night, yesterday's
Shop front broken.
Untangle the lies, then convincingly spoken,
Yeah, it's crazy alright,
And it's sick,
Like they're joking.
'Cos I thought;
If it's true,
If this planet is choking,
They'd be steering us clear
Least,
That's what I was hoping.

They're green-washing you, man
Lame creative accounting.
To encourage this path of
Consumption.
Amounting to
Bequeathing disaster,
Existential dangers
By corralling opinion
Via crude,
Echo chambers.

But our sun will come up,
This night's days are now numbered.
Our grandchildren,
Our hope,
Their new light, unencumbered.
For them, pure survival,
Cleaning up from the party.
They'll soon learn what we did,
Count our legacy
Harshly.

So we can close these tired eyes and
Not force them to open,
Stumble on and deny
That old systems are broken.

cont.

But when she reaches for me,
Platitudes won't suffice;
Grandfather / Granddaughter,
My choices / Her life.

Delilah

I saw the light through the night, as I parked by our window.
I saw our flickering telly aglow through the blind.
She'd signed a contract.
I went straight into our lounge, but stepped out of my mind.

Why, why, why, Delilah?
Sky! Sky! Sky! Delilah!
She could see, those channels were no good for me,
Plus I had issues with Murdoch that no one could see.

Then, the next day when I came home quite late she was waiting.
Collapsed in my chair, I just wanted to watch Final Score.
She stood there laughing,
But saw the remote in my hand, so she laughed no more.

Why, why, why, Delilah?
Prime! Prime! Prime! Delilah!
So, before this TV gets thrown at the wall,
Forgive me Delilah, I just couldn't take anymore.

She stood there laughing,
But saw the remote in my hand, so she laughed no more.

Why, why, why, Delilah?
Prime and Sky! Delilah!
So once more, our telly's in bits on the floor,
Forgive me Delilah, I just couldn't take anymore.
Forgive me Delilah, I just couldn't take anymore!

The Alibi

9 to 5

What an eventful week for Welsh rugby and for me it was topped off in a visitation by Dolly Parton in the dead of night (Liz is very understanding), so I had no choice but to do this.

But before we get into it, a word of support for the would-be striking Welsh rugby squad. It must be very hard to realize a life-long ambition, to become a full time professional athlete in your chosen field. Even more difficult than to be selected to represent your country, to wear the shirt, to reach the summit ...only to find that there is a kind of debt to repay and your side of a deal to fulfil. The WRU, having invested enormously in your particular region (and therefore in your personal development), require something in return; That you stick around for a specified time, 60 appearances under that global spotlight being that very agreement, thereby motivating and inspiring the next generation of boys and girls in that region of your country to reach for those same heights. There, I'm done ...well actually no, not quite.

To threaten, as one, to NOT fulfil those contractual obligations; to threaten en masse not to play IN A GAME OF RUGBY - FOR WALES; the readiness to deny ordinary folk who don't find themselves in such a vastly privileged position and for whom fixtures such as this are a much needed distraction from the very real difficulties of very real daily lives, in a transparent attempt to use the slipstream of public support for striking teachers, NHS staff, firefighters and public servants all at their wits end, with the primary objective of backing your employer into an impossible corner (who you'll recall financially supported you for all those years and without which, would have consigned you to playing your game for enjoyment, in what spare time you might have had, for recreation and for fun (remember that!)), is akin to wanting the penny and the bun and the bakery and options on the bakery to turn it into a more profitable nail bar. There. Over to you Dolly...

Tumble out of bed
And stumble in the kitchen,
Protein shake with kale and some fish in,
Yawn and belch and try to come to life.
Jump on the coach and the blood starts pumpin',
Out on the pitch even props are a-jumpin'
For folks like me on the job from 3 to 5.

Workin' 3 to 5,
What a way to make a livin'.
Sometimes get to fly,
But never club-class, it's demeaning!
They say, *never mind,*
But you know that they don't mean it.
It's enough to drive you
Crazy if you let it.

3 to 5,
Four Pernods then demotion,
You would think that I
Would have caused some big commotion.

cont.

Want to move abroad,
But the boss won't seem to let me.
I swear, the WRU's
Out to get me, hmmm.

They let you dream,
Just to watch them shatter.
You're just a notch on the Union's ladder,
But you speak to teams a long way away.
In the same squad with a lot of your friends,
Waitin' for the day your agent'll ring,
Then the tide's gonna turn
And the dosh is gonna roll your way!

Workin' 3 to 5,
What a way to make a livin'.
Rarely get a try,
It's all kickin', ain't no givin'.
And it's so unfair,
'Coz I never get the credit.
It's enough to drive you
Crazy if you let it.

3 to 5
Oh, what a way to make a living!
And there's no blind side,
It's all kickin', ain't no givin'.
We're so slow out there,
That we never get to spread it.
It's enough to drive you
Crazy if you let it.
etc. etc. etc...

COME ON WALES!

About the Author

Rob Kersley was born in Usk, Wales and was educated at Wern Secondary Modern School and Mid-Gwent College, Pontypool. He worked as a carpenter/joiner, surveyor, manager, operations director and managing director before re-evaluating and re-training as a deep tissue therapist.

He then established himself as the sole practitioner of a well-respected and successful deep tissue therapy practice near Brecon from 2003 until 2018 before relocating with his wife Liz to Cornwall where his daughter had settled some years earlier.

He joined Coast FM in Penzance as a presenter in 2019 to host a weekly radio show covering non-mainstream, contemporary artists and their music from around the globe. For some years he had been writing poetry and posting his work under the title, "Honddu Valley Herald" but his poems were first published in book form in 2022, in version eight of Penny Authors. Having those poems published and seeing his work in print, woke an aspiration to publish his own books of art and poetry. This opportunity presented itself through Penny Authors, to fulfil a lifelong dream.

His first book, "Time and Tide", and his second, "Factory Settings", were well received and the positive feedback from these books, together with increased following of his Honddu Valley Herald posts inspired him further. The thrilling realization that his very personal observations formulated in poetry were touching so many others, gave him the confidence to express even more about life and love; proclaim even more candidly his own failings and deepened his willingness to expose more of himself to the reader. Making this conscious decision to increase his vulnerability was as liberating as it was terrifying, but the result was a greater level of integrity and a more intimate transparency in his work.

A number of his poems are social reflections and some are political examinations, and yet Rob Kersley has *zero love of politics,* but rather *a total adulation of humanity and of the natural world*. However, since the critical decisions that effect these are inevitably political, an interrogation of these policies, the motivation behind them and of the people in charge, he sees as a necessity. He views his exploration of these issues, a matter of social responsibility rather than a fascination with politics and politicians for their own sake. It is his firm belief that choosing not to engage from this central element of life is a fundamental weakness of democracy in the twenty-first century. To that end, one of the key aims of his writing, of his poetry and of The Alibi, is to motivate and to inspire; to encourage positive and sincere engagement in life.

Also by Rob Kersley
From ArtNut/MAPublisher

1. Time and Tide published 2022

2. Factory Setting, published 2023

Both books are widely available around the world, Australia, Canada, Europe, UK and USA in on-line platforms, such as Lulu, Waterstones, Amazon and many others. You can also order them in your local bookshops.

For more information about the author and his books, please visit www.robkersley.uk, where you can order signed copies of the book.

www.ingramcontent.com/pod-product-compliance
Lightning Source LLC
Chambersburg PA
CBHW041247240426
43669CB00027B/2998